A Year in the Bull-Box

A Year in the Bull-Box
A POEM SEQUENCE
Glyn Hughes

PUBLICATIONS
2011

Published by Arc Publications
Nanholme Mill, Shaw Wood Road
Todmorden OL14 6DA, UK
www.arcpublications.co.uk

Copyright © Glyn Hughes 2011
Design by Tony Ward
Printed in Great Britain by the
MPG Book Group, Bodmin & King's Lynn

978 1906570 78 1 pbk
978 1906570 79 8 hbk

ACKNOWLEDGEMENTS:
Some of the poems in this collection first appeared in
Tears in the Fence ('Flowers', 'The Climb', 'Radiants', In
'Fiddle Wood' and 'April'); *Acumen* ('Seventy, Not Out');
North ('Dream Room'); *Scintilla* ('Soul Rise'); *Salzburg
Review* ('Lamb Time', 'January Twentieth', 'Falling
Asleep In A Meadow', 'Homage' and 'Rainy Autumn
Day'); *Alhambra Poetry Calendar* ('Greenfly'); *Ambit*
'Rainy Autumn Day') and *Poetry & Audience* ('End-
game').

Cover painting: 'Twiston Beck, Sketch 1" (watercolour)
by Glyn Hughes, 2010

Supported by
ARTS COUNCIL
ENGLAND

Editor for the UK and Ireland: John W. Clarke

In 2009 I was diagnosed with lymphoma cancer. On one of my first nights in the Huddersfield oncology ward, I dreamed that a wall-clock at the foot of my bed was replaced with a scroll covered in runes. I had to decipher these in order to regain health. On waking, I instantly understood. There were three parts to my recovery. One was medical attention. The second was my mental attitude. The third lay in my spiritual strength.

I had recently acquired use of an isolated stone hut (the "Bull-Box") in the Ribble Valley. The time spent there was my healing.

I dedicate this book to those who are helping me through by showing me so much that is positive and kindly – my consultants, the staff of the Calderdale Royal Hospitals and the Macmillan Centre, the friends and neighbours who earnestly help me with practical difficulties, the owners of the Bull-Box who allow me its use, and most of all to Elizabeth Lee who devotes herself to my care. I thank those who carefully advised on drafts of this book – especially David Pownall, Luke & Val Spencer, Ed Reis, John Fuller, and my editors at Arc, Tony Ward and Angela Jarman.

I also dedicate it to the vulnerable creatures, wild and domesticated, whom I have loved in the vicinity of my Bull-Box.

Contents

I

Bull-Box

I have acquired all the furniture I need
and left it behind, done all my repairs
and bought enough clothes.
The less you possess, the more they are
not decorations but what is more needed: icons
requiring as icons do small space to give up their worth –
this water jug, this stove, this lamp, this spade,
this small table and chair.
All of it "junk" in any place but here

                              in this hut
so tender in my feelings that when I turn the corner
I fear it might have proved a chimera,
a space among nettles, the victim of vandals.
For the dream is frail, yet firm the stone
of what is called "The Bull-Box" and that has held
one beast or another for a hundred years
so traditional is it, stone roof, stone walls,
no guttering, no drain-pipe, nettles rising to
a half-door and a square window
that look onto a half-moon meadow
seeded with wild wheat to a curve of stream.

                    In the sun
I watched a trout leap, a silver sword
small, quick, cutting air
as I built steps out of brook-stones
dug a pool for my washing-water
and saw a red-backed shrike on the thorns
that are overgrown behind The Bull-Box.
I was immortal then, not seventy but
a lithe, inquisitive
child again.

II
WINTER

Escape

In my first escape I was aged five or six
observing larks above a bristle of corn.
When following oracles in the countryside
I seemed to pass through a pane of glass
and feel an inner rising, as a lark in a field
that is a clod of earth until it sings
and sprays horizons with its song.

Salmon in Twiston Beck

Life is beginning again. In twilit winter
the messengers swim poking and feeling out of Nature
as under the skim of rain-clouded beck two salmon,
ghosts that recently held power
against an ocean, return to die in their known bourn.
Firstly under the coverlet of hurrying water
in their coupling they lie.

With their sacrifice and last fling
they have come into my world
yet leave a chink into theirs that shows
I am not the owner of my planet
even in imagination: the salmon
are too different. Yet the salmon's
log-like sickness couples with my own
while cancer-blood does its bad work on my eyes.

Yet in the virtue of sight before it dies
I have come into my self, my joy
on this edge where death's blindness surely
will peer into another life
in the small rest of night's sleep
in the longer rest of winter
and in the long, last rest of all.

White

1.

Frost came to conquer through the night
in a stillness that morning woke to.
After their over-eating, drinking fest
families that slipped away from Christmas
in The Old Schoolhouse, Old Chapel, The Old Post Office
(seasonal lights sprinkled like a promise of flowers)
to exercise children and dogs at last,
when they reached the cliff-top that pitches
deep into woods were amazed into silence.
For the dogs I suppose it was with cold
while children who also had never seen
such magic were in awe
like a first day at school, and the numbed adults
worked cameras. But where were the birds?
They could not be dead for there were no corpses.
They could not be hiding for there was nowhere to hide
and birds do not sleep long, they wake hungry,
their stomachs are small, they are not
furred animals deep in ice-plugged holes.

As the earth hugged itself tight
every frond was white-weighed and the woods
held a frost-hang. Splashings of streams
were icicles, the river was burnished black
and around the corner came a cloak
of ice-fog so timeless that one imagines
rising out of it the last great elk.

2.

Of course one must speak when one meets on a path
as narrow as this over rocks. Something portentous?
Not for nothing was this named "Hell Hole Rocks"
in the Age of Sermons. A place for casting down
just as many must have slipped here in the past.
Children who were too much children to be sure-footed
on the track down to work in quarry or mill
and men still morning-drunk from the hill-top village
all tumbled unredeemed.
A seat for Ascension also, as the Wesleys had it
who often spread their arms here, dressed in white. Yes,
one cannot just step aside smiling,
stirring the white powder off the grass.
"Who'd a thought it could be so beautiful"
whispered between strangers is not cliché but sharing
and a shared eye for beauty overcomes frost.

3.

Mind you, the cold teaches one to wait,
to pause over fires while the frost silence
deepens. Then to move quickly,
surprised at how lovely is the enduring cold
after rooms have become a hindrance;
the desk, the tasks
and the computer buzz that deafens out the birds
who sooner or later flicker and show they believe in life.

They show it by what one has missed; bright wings,
or the dark shooting-stars of fieldfares with hard voices,
and the woodpecker that calls from the wood.
The streams will sing between white crystals
nudging bulbs and roots.
Gold will appear or at any rate the tawny
bleached fields will emanate pale light.
Stillness will be over and the drenchings come that
have no resting place, yet smother everywhere.

At last there shall be flowers. Then will sprout
the jewels to focus our contemplation –
crocus and snowdrop
that are also white.

Greenfly

A greenfly sits on the uncomprehended glass
in uncomprehended light where the warmth pours.
To defend its untouchable, fragile beauty
in spanking-new green, look!
It has no less than four proboscises: two
small ones twitching constantly
and two that are graceful, longer than its body.
Black eyes glowing, each larger than its head.

How could such delicacy survive this frost?
If a child was sent out in that dress
the hours of parental stitching and pleating
would not last an hour in the garden

yet this fly
could be William Blake's model for that flying soul
he drew in delicate pencil, as if it might blow
away on the breeze of a hasty God.

Rooks

At last rooks and yet more rooks are shaking
voices that sound like a bagful of stones
the flock is dragging through the valley air
upstream at dawn and downstream at dark
so it must be Spring with the first grubs stirring
to be plucked at the valley-head from a ploughing

and the last winter wind has scattered
sticks along the wood and the lane-sides
as if on purpose for them to repair nests,
to quarrel and bicker in their zest for life
where the rookery stands. The attention-seeking *clack,*
the circling, and the homing search.

A Betwixt-and-Between Day

It seems another old day in dripping Winter.
Trees burned by cold are ashes, whips, or feathers
dipped out of gold mist and over damp-glazed leaves.
Yet a trembling of air is felt today
like invisible motions of a transparent moth.
Drip, drip, goes the light. The pink sky. The blue snow –
thawing, though. Pigeons are mating over light snow.
Plants break through: suns burning with a green light.
Brilliance of wet evergreen, harts-tongue fern
and of crowded, or crushed, mossed boughs
where moor and wood shade down to the stream
which is hardly colours for the plaited light
of water steals it. – Leaves of wild garlic
from which I'll soon make soup, appear.
Watercress, from which I will also make soup, but that is best raw.

                                   Oh, here comes a cliff of rain!
Soon horse, and turned-out cat, and cattle –
all that have lost the wildness to protect themselves
or hide – grow drooped and sodden.

    *

Entwined hedgerows, nightshade and honeysuckle
is where the hazel now flowers
(yellow but not bright yellow of pollen yet)
and the wind snaps through unleafed gaps.

Birdsong breaks as they change their habits.
Paired finches separate from flocks.
Ravelling and unravelling skeins of geese –
– tossed rosaries – fly up from the estuary.
Blackbirds carry-on in thorn bushes

and robins sing even at night.
Such beguiling delicacy –
you would not think they'd be aggressive.
Ignorant too, with a faith
that magpies will not hunt their eggs.

Magpies will hop and leap the hedge-top
in a swearing gang of bandits
driving their knife-beaks through the pools of leaves
even to the eyes of nestlings.

And this is as truly Spring
as all that nonsense of *hey-nonny-no*.

Cyclamens

Wild, wing-petalled cyclamens,
winter flowers that seem part butterfly
or angel; of earth, yet only for a moment settled
or rather, hovering, about to fly again –
both winged and lightly anchored.

Life's purpose seems for this
moment that is entirely itself;
is all that I can know – I know.
All life, dammed behind,
means nothing but that it led to this.

III
SPRING

Homage

I am plain and plebeian among the robed ones.
Plumaged souls they are,
weightless voices in the trees
at dawn and dusk especially.
Hardly bigger than raindrops
they are the alpha and omega of my days.
Humbled by their extravagance
of fight sometimes, or sweetness, and of flight
my tiny life looks up to them, with my little hold on song.

Lamb Time

He has been in this world for one whole day
so knows all about it or as much
as anything can in the strangeness of entering.
For instance the oddity of humans
that he runs from his mother to inspect
then after her steady, melancholy bleat
comes to a halt with a perfect brake
uncertain at being so curious (he inspects
with his nose a thistle's rosette).

Men will come with dogs and predatory heartlessness –
but mothers are not always right after all –
so he changes his mind. That change of mind
of itself, it seems, brings panic and haste
back to the teat, in his Heaven above him. His sky,
the belly above him. He arches backwards then,
until she grows impatient and kicks him away.

Falling Asleep In A Meadow

As Spring comes on, again I remember,
after a morning that was laid under dew
which a week ago would have been frost,
as I lie among it then wake again
in its melt of harmonising sound –
as it comes out of its own sleep brimming with song –
the great chorus of Nature.
      Wake at first feeling soft and lost
in the sun, contentment and discontent undecided
while the contemplative feelings disperse
through what fine siftings
as far as the blackbird in the far wood

now not merely watchful
but part of the honey-bee at the flower
and of the eager, hungry bird
as all that was anxious drains away down what
ducts of the Imagination
we had forgotten
would save us from our restless selves.

All afternoon we will sit here in peace,
we will sit or lie here all the afternoon.

A Thrush Struck My Window.

1.

What has settled the sun's uproar, the clamour
of lambs, of farmers sawing logs upon the dam's
bank of wild garlic and primroses
(I think I could hear the joy of flowers
competing to outshine the sun) –
piercing of song from fierce whitethroat and wren –
yesterday was unexpected rain in the night
and dawn waking to a voluminous quiet
but for a thrush that drew back the rain's
hiss across woods that are curtains of brown silk
in the grey damp of this morning that wakes me.

2.

With a thud the loud songster from the wood
strikes the glass and in his pre-death stun
is patient as he must be, winking
the cold-seeming, blue-grey lid of his eye;
his dark-brilliant spots heaving like explosive black suns.

Can I, should I rescue him,
force milk into that gasping beak
as I did with hurt birds when I was a child?
They always died, no doubt their fear
caused by me, worsened their chances.
I leave him panting in his sunny place; his enemies,
jackdaws and crows that colonise the wych-elm
are away foraging.

Soul Rise

Hedge-tops are stooped with their flower burden,
hawthorn and first rose. Fields are all buttercups, sorrel
and flowering grass before being made into hay.
                                    Walk slowly for that is to give
in looks and pauses, the soul its room.
It touches each branch and bird.

In fact you now feel that it is what you are.
Have become before a flower, a room of the soul.
Nothing else accounts for this harmony
and away from the tempting awe of this sight
each further step seems treachery.

Mistress

who gardens my inner world
that its secrets might flower as they should –
Delphic and cave-throned
in the hollow out of which all dreams come,
you have settled in the shade of orchard trees
at the Calf's Head with your two or three
glasses of wine and the Sunday papers

until I – a restless walker – will
return, like some male Flora,
bringing, while the light is good,
wild flowers dipped in streams to freshen them
for you.

IV
SUMMER

June

Have you seen how a whitethroat, tossed here on winds,
a hundred feathers weighing no more than one, sings?

From claws upwards it thrusts into that poise,
a balanced aim for that open beak
scissoring the air with bird-scales,
throwing them sideways as it twirls
down branches, never failing.
It cannot help but spill its song.

Listen. When the whitethroat sinks into the wood
because though treading quietly one has startled it
or a shadow that could be a hawk has unsettled it
the song with which it did not hesitate
grows louder, magnified from the heart of trees.

Thus here I sing,
gently arriving. Then the mind quickens to its purpose
while creatures bless me with disregard.

Flowers

Hedgerows are pricked with the lights of roses
of such incandescence that they seem to burst
into fire and lose substance
so that mere hands pass through them.

At one point Keats thought his only happiness
had come from looking at flowers.
Sometimes I too think that the one light
I followed was through the garden,
in trance to the brief yet inexhaustibly supplied
flames that I'd liken to the beauty of angels

at this hour when what they are attuned to is the song
of thrush and robin at dawn.
Then all seems a harmony of the spheres
in a green light (which is the grasses' part,
honoured by fading stars).

Flowers give the light back in cups of beauty.
They recompense the dark
and bandage the damaged soul.

Two Heifers

I am half asleep in their field when two heifers,
one part Ayrshire, patched brown,
one Friesian, stumble across their meadow,
fumble out of the aeons
with what grace has been granted by humans;
holding onto what remains from the ages of breeding
that was not for their good, holding onto what pride
is left them. Their young bodies
already seem to be heaving bags of stones,
a promise of weight and awkwardness.

They pause a few feet off, curious. Delicately
turning from a confusing surprise –
a human asleep among fodder and flowers –
one gently licks the neck of the other
who submits head-lowered as a newborn daughter.

She continues to stroke with her strong, dark tongue.
She rasps the long face, cheek and eyes,
their peat-brown beauty running with the damage of flies
still hovering over her knotted brow.

                        The motherly one tires
and turns to the grass. The licked one, the more delicate
Ayrshire, questions her sister,
nuzzling with tender awareness.

              My moment with them is also a singular
time among the herds,
glad to have awoken among cattle and flowers.

Salmon Parr

Full summer and a sheen on seeded grass.
Fields of buttercup and sorrel, eyed with the blue
of forget-me-not by the river bank
where in dark pools are ghosts seen by few.

Salmon parr five inches long
lurk in coiled shoals, under roots and stones
where a thousand eggs were laid from the adult pair just strong
enough to winnow the gravel on their death's eve last December.

Sometimes they foolishly bask in the sun
away from the shoal or inexpertly snap at flies.
These lights out of the depth-dark vanish at sight
for if they do not flick back fast as light they are prey to heron
or kingfisher which have appeared.
But mostly they are spectres under the ripples' shades.

To glimpse them through their shy deception
is to catch for a moment maybe one tenth
of their vast lives.
            Only we sense that such shadows of water-shadows
lurk under the same surface where our thoughts
that we might have spoken if one could grasp them, vanish.

Monday Without End

Let me show you later today
through a haze of wine outdoors and the heat,
meadows not yet mown and in their glory.
Orchids, seeded grass and sorrel.

Art can convey but it cannot give
unless each artwork carried a phial
of meadow scent and not even then
though I would like this poem to have one
holding the smell of cattle, clover, and drying hay
as I wait for you to come home.

IV
AUTUMN

Radiants

When the larks fly off –
not singly ascending but, at summer's end,
nests abandoned, in a flock
swift, low over fields –
tiles of light are scattered on their wings
as if a brightness up there has been shattered.

I fancy that in such scraps of light
our insights come, the grace of words.
Like an old church window perhaps,
smashed by the envious worldly,
its fragments lying in muck on the floor.
Or a bright river glimpsed through trees:
eyes in a quiver of wind,
water rippling after, out of shade.

The Climb

Thread your way between the houses
at one side, the gorge deeper and noisier
with wind and water on the other
and turn to climb a silent valley
deep in leaf-mould, with falling
or fallen trees in an autumn shroud.
Maybe a robin startles depths
with its song or rather with a sweet lament.
Otherwise, silence thickens.

In your breathless stumbling
you wonder why you are doing this
until you break out on the lip of rocks
and are un-shrouded again by light and wind
that earlier disturbed a roof of trees.
Your breath quite differently taken away.

In Fiddle Wood

When I went into the wood
it was still for an hour in its autumn collapse.
No leaf fell while I was there
they hung on delicately as spiders to their webs
poised and patient – the gold, the crimson perhaps
and ones of emerald that some think sickly.
Trees so filled with gold give out a light. The brook
before reaching the mill is scattered with light,
with eddies where sky, slate-blue, breaks in to look.
Clouds' silver breaks through the mossed boughs
fallen too thickly even for deer.

                The sun carved this perfected silence
and it was a surprise
as the ordinary should be. I hardly wished or dared another step
unsure that one perfection could replace another
yet each movement presented one to my eyes
and then another, shot with light.

Of course there is no such thing as stillness.
It would rain tomorrow, maybe in an hour
or in five minutes, making watercolours of my notes.
Temporary exhaustion is what I witnessed.
Winter, a bedding down for renewal. But when all will be cold
and trees bare of cluttering summer, truth will be seen.

Then I turned indeed towards some rain
although the heart of the wood
was still a cocoon within wind-sound, the flutes and moans
tipping high branches.
              I faced the whispered shudders of it,

light but nevertheless leaf-flinging;
a shimmer of noisy stars
that even flooded the distant and so-tidy cottages
with their discreet lamps alight on the edge of the wood.

*

One month later
wind in undammed torrents has threshed the trees
and a frost-mist, rushing in wisps sucked higher,
weaves the morning boughs.
                    Sun arcs low now over the Wood,
its track a scythe-blade through its frozen fires.
The steep wood is velvet. The mill walls, blackberry-black.
Tree shadows are white. The walls' shadows are white
patches of frost saved in the thawed gold
of fields that have slow-burned their way through frost.
Hunger of birds' shouts in the blue air
that has advanced over the dawn.
What can they find, those rooks and that dark, cold
blackbird skimming the stream?
Hunger incarnate is a small beast or bird turning leaves
that rattle with frost.

Though they have spun cloth – and came here to dance
with fiddles before the age of the mills – they have not lived here,
except for paupers' children brought in to weave,
carted from no-one cared where, and immured.
Perhaps they peered through barred windows at this beauty...
they must have done, when others shunned it,

and not only because this is "The Dark Side"
for nine months a year.
                          And yet I love the spirits
which, for good or ill,
one looks everywhere over one's shoulder for
but especially in the abandoned mill
ghoulish with its hoods of livid moss.

Rainy Autumn Day

It is in this light that every sadness descends
as if it was always at this time that lovers left you
or you left them. Arguments led to departures
when nights drew in and roads like this
lit at this hour only one week previously
were dark and wet and splattered with brown
or black leaves, your headlights bouncing
on a new strangeness. In this light
as a boy you were sure of being
like Van Gogh or Mozart, and would not live to enjoy it.
Yes, this is their light really;
not all that sun, not those courtly chandeliers.

Two On A Bridge

She with thrust breasts and blonde coiffure
was seventy if a day, and he an old man scrubbed
down to his consuming smile –
though not for her (they were shy in their new love)
but for the ducks;
both unable to believe their luck
at a chance for another self.

One to see themselves as they seemed not
until they met, yet also seeing
that they are now what they always knew they were.

Seventy, Not Out

I'll keep my stick. I also want
a four-wheel drive, off-roader,
souped-up invalid-chair
with a three-litre engine to climb the hills
where later they may scatter my ashes
as curlews and peewits dance on the air;
a stereo to play Bach's *Mass in B Minor*
and a flashing light such as doctors have,
saying "poet on call". Thus I'll park anywhere
at the muse's house. The stick is to wave
at anyone who objects to me, "Out of my hair!"

Village Haven

How and when did it occur
that we grew into a tribe of ailing elders
loving to gossip in the street
where village traffic is courteous,
we savouring – if hardly revelling in –
our strata of convictions laid-down by place and neighbours?

The happiest that a person can be,
some think, is adjusted to a small community;
that narrow gullet where the salmon
returns to breed and die in its birth channel.

                    Others go about their business
which I observe in the lazy way a person
passes a slack line into an ocean
or savours eddies

puzzled by the shallows of our lives,
also by its leaps of joy
knowing only faith, fantasy, fear and hope
of death, until the last act which is not death, but *dying*.

Going There On The Long Causeway

There are cottages up there with boulders before their doors.
Stone is the beauty of here, its forms, its shine,
its glitter of silica in rain, or laid across fields
and some stones are as large as churches;
the Pennines' unavoidable substance.
"Here lies this stone that waits the Resurrection"
as one in Elland churchyard has it.
Some cottages are so decrepit and embittered where they crouch
that they seem to be ancient, whole stones themselves
though of course they were built where they are for shelter –
as the mind also shelters behind a conviction
or a Bible crumpled with old wisdom until it is mouldy.

And I see at his door a stubborn man, one bowed before his time;
not loved by wife, I suspect, nor children and no wonder;
who has given up on love
and who attempts to lever the stone of his life for another try
where it lodges fast again: this stone of wintry grief
soon to be a perch for the curlew to spring from and cry,
riding its wet currents over "the tops".
This stone could be the pedestal for any sky-journey,
the wild bird tells us with a high, soprano call
as I drive past slowly to reach my Paradise.

*

I once walked here for days because of what matched it in my mind.
Even then I could not help thinking that mine was a collective grief,
as small stones together pave a road
and that here seem almost to pave the air

for a journey that was expected and yet not prepared for.
I was going to the place all art and poetry reaches
on the journey of dying, unprepared for until we need it.
Then thoughts like dreams sink back to the place we'd rather not visit,
or rather not stay when we have been.
Where unlike at first birth no-one celebrates our coming.

So let this stone of grief laid sooner or later be
not the cover of a tomb but a pedestal
for the curlew's Spring call
to a sky-trip clean across the valleys of Padiham and Burnley.

Endgame

The green lane, higher deeper than it is wide
and so narrow that only the smaller carts
could rattle along in tune with the dry song of the yellowhammer,
the iron grinding on stone through almost a tunnel
so that even standing on shafts one could hardly look over –
there were many such lanes. This one survives
the same as in earliest years when it led me
in childhood snaking from home.
Perhaps the first green of hawthorn was the most beautiful.
Or specks of white stitchwort buds
dropped, (it seemed), on banks of thickening grass.
The campions that were blood specks, emerging too.
But what about summer when the hawthorns flowered?
Or the yellowhammer that bounced onto the hedge-top from the field?
In age it is the same, drawing me excitedly,
the eye of my silence watching as always,
the ear of silence listening.

At the end of the lane
 being lost is of no account. Leading anywhere or nowhere
it spreads through a land stacked with primrose cowslip.
And here I am recalling the young ghost that is still me,
welcomed by light and by whatever has bloomed overnight.
So here I am
in the not stark but beautiful lanes of endgame.
Whether leading anywhere or nowhere, yet they spread into lands
that are anything but desolate. Beauty abounds.
There amongst fields and nameless lanes are small shelters
and someone runs each with kindness. Don't ask for more.

VI

Night In The Cancer Ward

The bedside lamp, my spectacles, glass of water,
watch laid by, a stack of books;
and pain reliably hunting. Pain reliably hunting;
books; my watch laid by; my glass of water;
bedside lamp; and nurses walking. (Walking!)
This circles day by day, and I waiting
for someone.

Or could it be for *Someone*?
One night I dreamed of a woman, also of God;
God not seen – how can He be seen – but advising
her, my new spirit, to move in uncluttered.
Or perhaps it was actually Him, not merely dreamed of although
embodied in a dream?
Or am I delirious?

Switch on my lamp again at three
and listen to the grunts of sleepers.
It seems their souls have left them and purgatory lies
between day and day where breed dark evils and fears.
I have stared at their masked and almost-blinded faces
eight days now, moved by compassion
for those who might have revolted me some weeks ago.
That's a gift I needed and it came.

Angrily in his mother's tongue, the old Ukrainian
mutters in his sleep. (Of death camps?
Quelled fears of an *untermenschen*?)
Someone vomits. Another screams.
Deep in the wards, a telephone rings.
One limps to the bathroom dragging
his apparatus linked to the ante-room of death.

Thus time is spent in our timeless yet time-haunted place
through the trance of pain
where all have their ways of shamming cheerfulness
while I do not know what is happening in my body
as the drip-feed purrs at my side.
I am hungry for more life, but in me
circulates what is greedy for Death
and can I fight it? Has it been here long?

                              No point now
in looking back at the slipstream of my flights
of high, thin hope. This is to be animal again
alert for danger or I'll die
from the mystery that is stalking.

        *

The bedside lamp, the spectacles, the glass of water,
the books, and thoughts of places I hoped to visit:
all will vanish.
                    Nature goes off by herself, dancing,
too youthful for an interest in age and death.
I see through the window the flash of her green foot
skipping weightless into further green
as a Spring morning comes.

Bird song. And sunlight, making up for night's lost time
darts with shock in the trees...
I can sleep now.

Migrants

Rain is scurrying along the gutter.
It drops like living creatures – spiders, say –
and falls outside the window
slant-wise in a wet-loaded wind,
gleaming as cars do, beading the far hill,
that seem to kiss then pass and fall away.

And for months now through the winter weather,
like rising dust-storms or pale-winged handfuls of sand
flocks of pigeons have poured to and fro.

Disturbing, too, when birds resist,
slip under the wind:
tremors of being that face the elements
which one does not expect of such grains.

Dream Room

1.

My "dream room" I call it, at the top of the house.
Television's on downstairs: the News.
I could go down and try to work out who
hates who today and why
but is it worth it when they hate
not to be static and die?
I'm happiest in my room because through dreams
I find what I never knew I was.
I think I could get out,
catch trains, crash lanes or go abroad
but it would be to dream about my room.

2.

The ghost soaked into the walls of my room
emerging at dawn when I enter
is my younger self that thought it *chose*
to dwell here thirty years ago.
As I look out of the window it is the ghost
of youth that loves those depths of light and shade,
horses dappling through them, and the flick of birds.

I invite only one to my room: my inner being.
Bedraggled as an old sheep-dog from wandering,
black with moor-dirt as if he's been down the pit,
he takes off his coat as though he owns the place
and exhausts his host with revelations.

3.

The ghost whispers in my ear,
"You are setting off again with some old friend,
Dave, Peter, Raymond, or a woman you knew
and married." Rucksacks packed – I see those ghosts —
we pass through the tall grasses
dried, soaked once more; rank and pungent.

And there is your younger self again
peering at the usually un-regarded.

4.

A house is a symbol of a poet's mind
and mine is a tower, though not like Yeats's.
Three cottages on a hillside – three weavers' families –
were once stacked here in a sooty light.

Now from the pink blotting of dawn
to the yellow-brown sky of burned metal threatening storm
heat owns the day. My room under the slates
is the quiet ante-room to purgatory

where I wait among the demons
of sins and mistakes burning through memory
seeking to be free of the karmic needs
escaped, but never resolved, through beauty:

flowering heather and gorse upon the common
in their miraculous duet
of purple and yellow, a sun-catching glow.

   5.

If all the feelings that I ever had
are congregated in this room –
spirits like moths after a hot night
that have stumbled in with beating wings
(as if wings were their very hearts in the dark)
and settled, wings dusty, folded,
faking dead but they can be touched into life

then each new singled-out affection
from the past and now flying again
will alter the world – as they did the first time –

so that when I step into the morning
receiving the pink spreading and brightening on my eyes
I am more blessed than yesterday.

Biographical Note

GLYN HUGHES lives in West Yorkshire, a place that has inspired much of his work. He also lived for a long period in Greece. His first full collection of poetry, *Neighbours* (1970) was a Poetry Book Society Recommendation and won the Arts Council of Wales Poetry Prize. It was followed by further collections: *Rest The Poor Struggler* (1972); and *Best of Neighbours: New & Selected Poems* (1979); *Dancing Out of the Dark Side (2005);* and *Life Class* (2009).

His first novel was *Where I Used to Play on the Green* (1982), winner of the *Guardian* Fiction Prize and the David Higham Prize for Fiction. It was followed by further novels, *The Hawthorn Goddess* (1984); *The Rape of the Rose* (1987); *The Antique Collector* (1990), set in the Pennines and short-listed for the 1990 Whitbread Novel Award; *Roth* (1992); and *Brontë* (1996), a fictionalised life of the Brontë family.

His books, *Millstone Grit* (1975), revised and republished as *Millstone Grit: A Pennine Journey* (1987), *Fair Prospects* (1976) and *Glyn Hughes' Yorkshire* (1985) are works of autobiography. He is also the editor of *Samuel Laycock: Selected Poems* (1981).

He has written a number of plays for stage (*Mary Hepton's Heaven*, 1984), television and radio, including three verse plays for children. His other radio plays are *Pursuit, Mr Lowry's Loves, Glorious John, When Twilight Falls* and *Dreams of a Working Man*, all produced for Radio 4 in Birmingham. His radio features include *The Red Room* (about Charlotte Brontë), *Millstone Grit Revisited* and *The Long Causeway*, a series about crossing the Pennines.

He has performed his work world-wide. He is a former Arts Council Fellow, and has held Writer in Residence positions at Bishop Grosseteste College, Lincoln, at Farnborough Library, Hampshire, and for the D. H. Lawrence Centenary Festival, Nottingham.

Glyn Hughes is also a painter and has exhibited widely in the North of England.

Recent titles in Arc Publications'
POETRY FROM THE UK / IRELAND,
include:

LIZ ALMOND
The Shut Drawer
Yelp!

D M BLACK
Claiming Kindred

JAMES BYRNE
Blood / Sugar

JONATHAN ASSER
Outside The All Stars

DONALD ATKINSON
In Waterlight: Poems New,
Selected & Revised

ELIZABETH BARRETT
A Dart of Green & Blue

JOANNA BOULTER
Twenty Four Preludes & Fugues on
Dmitri Shostakovich

THOMAS A CLARK
The Path to the Sea

TONY CURTIS
What Darkness Covers
The Well in the Rain
folk

JULIA DARLING
Sudden Collapses in Public Places
Apology for Absence

CHRIS EMERY
Radio Nostalgia

LINDA FRANCE
You are Her

KATHERINE GALLAGHER
Circus-Apprentice
Carnival Edge

CHRISSIE GITTINS
Armature

RICHARD GWYN
Sad Giraffe Café

MICHAEL HASLAM
The Music Laid Her Songs in Language
A Sinner Saved by Grace
A Cure for Woodness

MICHAEL HULSE
The Secret History

BRIAN JOHNSTONE
The Book of Belongings

JOEL LANE
Trouble in the Heartland
The Autumn Myth

HERBERT LOMAS
The Vale of Todmorden
A Casual Knack of Living
(COLLECTED POEMS)

PETE MORGAN
August Light

MICHAEL O'NEILL
Wheel

MARY O'DONNELL
The Ark Builders

IAN POPLE
An Occasional Lean-to
Saving Spaces

PAUL STUBBS
The Icon Maker

SUBHADASSI
peeled

LORNA THORPE
A Ghost in My House

MICHELENE WANDOR
Musica Transalpina
Music of the Prophets

JACKIE WILLS
Fever Tree
Commandments